The Best of Mary Maxim®

Bedtime Blankies

2

Easy-to-follow symbol charts guide you in making color changes that create adorable images on crochet baby afghans!

14

7

LEISURE ARTS, INC. • Maumelle, Arkansas

Rocking Ponies Blanket

INTERMEDIATE

SHOPPING LIST

Yarn (Worsted Weight) MEDIUM 4
[3.5 ounces, 180 yards
(100 grams, 165 meters) per ball]:

- ☐ Main Color - Pale Teal 7 balls
- ☐ Color 1 - Dk Teal 1 ball
- ☐ Color 2 - Camel 1 ball
- ☐ Color 3 - Dk Brown 70 yds
- ☐ Color 4 - White 1 ball

Crochet Hook

- ☐ Size J-10 (6.00 mm)
  or size needed for gauge

SIZE INFORMATION

Size: 35" x 43" [89 x 109 cm]

GAUGE INFORMATION

13 sc and 15 rows to 4" [10 cm] measured over single crochet using **suggested** hook or any size hook which will give the correct stitch gauge.

STITCH GUIDE

PC - Popcorn: Work 4 dc in stitch indicated, drop loop from hook, insert hook in first dc of group just made, then pick up dropped loop & draw through to close the Popcorn.

Entire afghan is worked in sc with some PC. Each square on the graph represents one st. Color changes are indicated with different symbols. Odd numbered rows or **right side rows** are worked from right to left and even numbered rows or **wrong side rows** are worked from left to right.

To change colors on ODD numbered rows (Right Side Facing): *Work across graph to st before new color, insert hook in next st and pull up a loop; join new color yarn and holding tail at back of work, yarn around hook and pull through 2 loops of previous color on hook.*

Notice that the st just made will be entirely in the first color and the loop on the hook in the new color, ready to make the next st. When ready for the next color change, rep from * to *.

Old colors are not to be carried across the back of work more than a few sts or you will not have sufficient yarn to complete the afghan. If sts on graph return to original color later in row, join on a separate ball of yarn. You may need to work with several colors at a time. For large areas of color, use different balls of yarn; for small areas, you can create bobbins of colors needed (allow about 20" [51 cm] for 10 sts). When area of color has been completed, cut yarn leaving a 3-4" [7.5-10 cm] tail to be woven in when afghan has been completed.

To change color on EVEN numbered rows (Wrong Side Facing): **Work across graph to st before new color, insert hook in next st and pull up a loop, bring strand of yarn to front to work; join new color yarn and holding tail at front of work, yarn around hook and pull through 2 loops on hook.**

NOTE: With both strands of yarn in front at this point, the next sc may be partially hidden - be careful not to skip a st by mistake. When ready for the next color change, rep from ** to **.

If color changes are made correctly, you will be able to see small "feathers" of yarn on the wrong side of work where the old color was brought to the front; but the right side should look quite neat and regular.

INSTRUCTIONS

Panel A: (make 2) Using MC, ch 34.

Now beg with a right side row, proceed to follow Graph A on page 6, working as follows.

Row 1: Sc in 2nd ch from hook and in each ch across - 33 sc.

Row 2: Ch 1, turn, sc in each sc across - 33 sc.

Continue to follow Graph A, working color design and Popcorns as indicated until 66 rows have been completed, then rep Rows 11-66 once more, then Rows 11-32 once.

Note: The 2 popcorns worked at top of heart are worked on wrong side, push through to front of blanket. Now work 10 rows, using MC only - total of 154 rows.

Do Not Fasten off.

Border:

Rnd 1: (wrong side facing) *Work 116 sc evenly along side edge of Panel, work 3 sc in next corner, work 31 sc evenly along short end, work 3 sc in next corner; rep from * once more, join - 306 sc. Break yarn and fasten off.

Rnd 2: Join White in last sc of last rnd, ch 1, sc in same st, sc in next sc, **working around next sc, insert hook into end of row on panel, draw up a long loop even with row being worked and complete sc as usual* - **Long sc made,** sc in each of next 3 sc; rep from * to center sc of next corner, work 3 sc in corner sc, sc in each of next 33 sc, 3 sc in corner sc**, sc in each of next 2 sc; rep from * once more, but ending last rep at **. Break yarn and fasten off.

To Make Panel B: (make 1) Using MC, ch 34.

Now beg with a right side row, proceed to follow Graph B on page 6, working as follows:

Row 1: Sc in 2nd ch from hook and in each ch across - 33 sc.

Row 2: Ch 1, turn, sc in each sc across - 33 sc.

Continue to follow Graph B, working color design and Popcorns as indicated until 66 rows have been completed, then rep Rows 11-66 once more, then Rows 11-32 once.

Note: The 2 popcorns worked at top of heart are worked on wrong side, push through to front of blanket. Now work 10 rows, using MC only - total of 154 rows.

Do Not Fasten off.

Border: Work as given for Panel A.

To Assemble: Take Panel A and Panel B, with right sides tog (make sure panels have bottom edges at the bottom), using White and working through back loops, sew panels tog.

Then sew second Panel A to other side of Panel B in the same manner.

Blanket Edging:

Rnd 1: With right side of blanket facing, join White in 3rd sc of upper corner, ch 1, sc in same st around, working 3 sc in each corner sc, changing to Dk Teal in last sc, join. Break White and fasten off.

Rnd 2: Using Dk Teal, ch 3 (counts as first dc), *dc in each sc to corner sc, (2 dc, ch 1, 2 dc) in corner sc; rep from * around, join with sl st in top of beg ch-3. Break yarn and fasten off.

Weave in all ends neatly.

GRAPH A

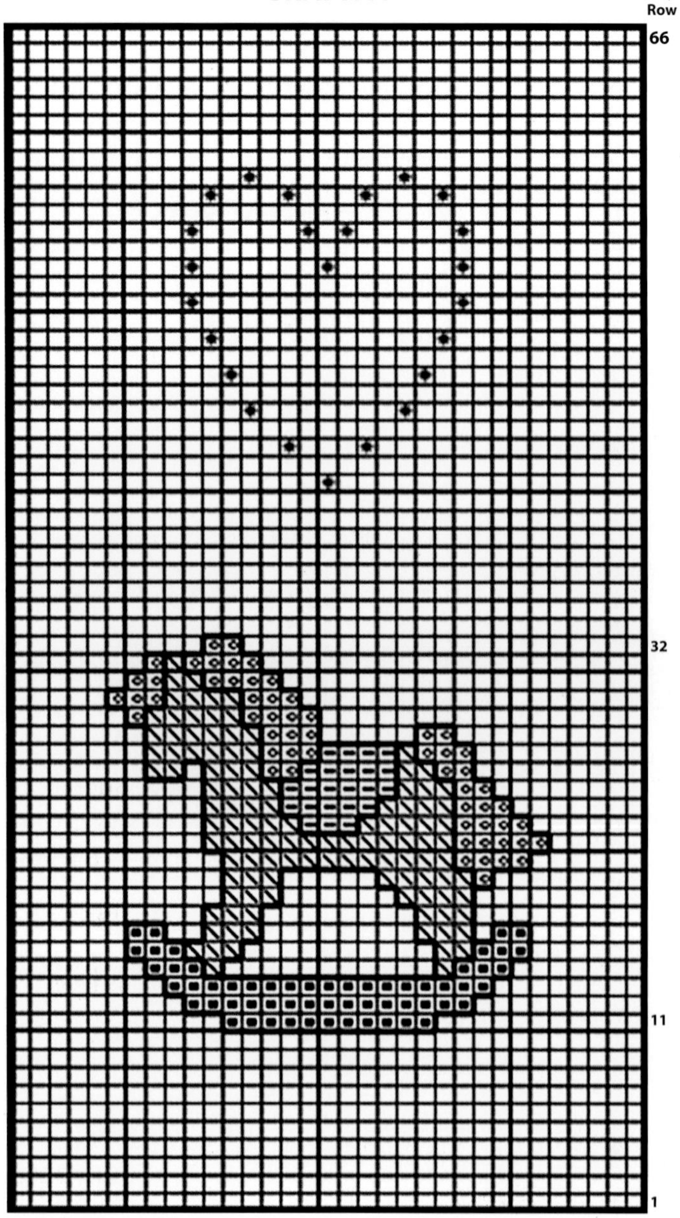

READ WRONG SIDE ROWS FROM THIS SIDE

READ RIGHT SIDE ROWS FROM THIS SIDE

GRAPH B

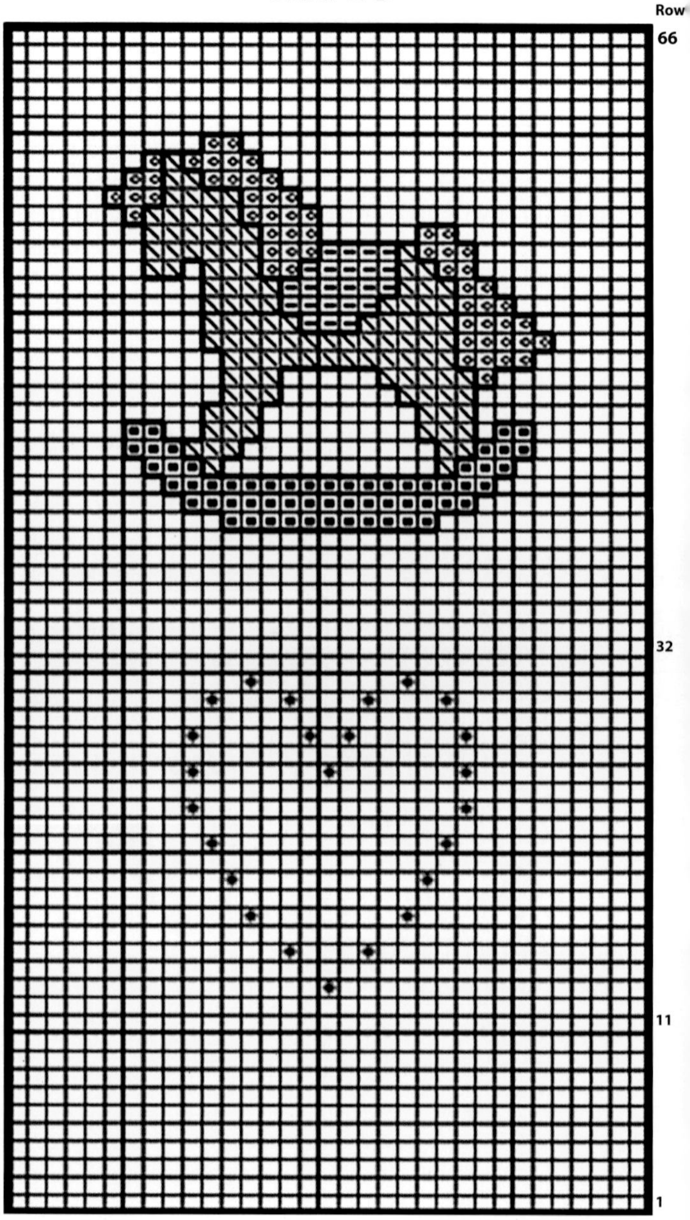

READ WRONG SIDE ROWS FROM THIS SIDE

READ RIGHT SIDE ROWS FROM THIS SIDE

STITCH GUIDE

MC ☐ Pale Teal
CC ■ Dk Brown
CC ╲ Camel
CC ○ White
CC ▬ Dk Teal
✱ Popcorn (see Stitch Guide on page 2)

Night Owls Blanket

INTERMEDIATE

SHOPPING LIST

Yarn (Worsted Weight)

MEDIUM 4

[3.5 ounces, 180 yards (100 grams, 165 meters) per ball]:

- ☐ Dk. Blue 3 balls
- ☐ Lt. Blue 3 balls
- ☐ Aqua 1 ball
- ☐ Camel 1 ball
- ☐ Natural 1 ball
- ☐ Silver Blue 1 ball
- ☐ Green 1 ball
- ☐ Brown 105 yds
- ☐ Dk. Brown 70 yds
- ☐ White 70 yds
- ☐ Taupe Ragg 70 yds
- ☐ Pale Brown 35 yds
- ☐ Dk. Yellow 35 yds
- ☐ Yellow 35 yds

Crochet Hook

- ☐ Size J-10 (6.00 mm) or size needed for gauge

SIZE INFORMATION

Size: 42" x 38" [106.5 x 96.5 cm]

GAUGE INFORMATION

13 sc and 15 rows to 4" [10 cm] measured over single crochet using **suggested** hook or any size hook which will give the correct stitch gauge.

STITCH GUIDE

Entire afghan is worked in sc. Each square on the graph represents one sc. Color changes are indicated with different symbols. Odd numbered rows or **right side rows** are worked from right to left and even numbered rows or **wrong side rows** are worked from left to right.

To change colors on ODD numbered rows (Right Side Facing): *Work across graph to st before new color, insert hook in next st and pull up a loop; join new color yarn and holding tail at back of work, yarn around hook and pull through 2 loops of previous color on hook.* Notice that the st just made will be entirely in the first color and the loop on the hook in the new color, ready to make the next st. When ready for the next color change, rep from * to *.

Old colors are not to be carried across the back of work more than a few sts or you will not have sufficient yarn to complete the afghan. If sts on graph return to original color later in the row, join on a separate ball of yarn. You may need to work with several colors at a time. For large areas of color, use different balls of yarn; for small areas, you can create bobbins of colors needed (allow about 20" [51 cm] for 10 sts). When area of color has been completed, cut yarn leaving a 3-4" [7.5-10 cm] tail to be woven in when afghan has been completed.

To change color on EVEN numbered rows (Wrong Side Facing): **Work across graph to st before new color, insert hook in next st and pull up a loop, bring strand of yarn to front of work; join new color yarn and holding tail at front of work, yarn around hook and pull through 2 loops on hook.**

NOTE: With both strands of yarn in front at this point, the next sc may be partially hidden - be careful not to skip a st by mistake. When ready for the next color change, rep from ** to **.

If color changes are made correctly, you will be able to see small "feathers" of yarn on the wrong side of work where the old color was brought to the front; but the right side should look quite neat and regular.

INSTRUCTIONS

Using Dark Blue, ch 131.

Foundation Row: Following Row 1 of Graph A on pages 10-11, sc in 2nd ch from hook and in each ch to end, ch 1, turn - 130 sc.

Next Row: Following Row 2 of Graph A (for color changes), work as follows: sc in first sc and in each sc to end, ch 1, turn - 130 sc.

Repeat last row, but continue to work through Graph A until 68 rows have been completed.

Beg with a right side row, proceed to follow Graph B on pages 12-13, working in the same manner, until 68 rows have been completed.

Fasten off. Weave in all ends.

Please Note: When working the border around the outside of the afghan, please note that it is not necessary to work a sc into each stitch at the ends of rows. This may cause the border to be wavy. This border was crocheted by skipping every 3rd or 4th stitch as needed.

Border:

Rnd 1: Using Dark Blue, with right side of blanket facing, join yarn in any corner. *Work 3 sc in corner, work in sc evenly to next corner; rep from * around afghan, join with slip st in beg sc.

Next Rnd: Ch 1, *3 sc in corner sc, sc in each sc to next corner; rep from * around, join with slip st in beg sc.

Repeat this last rnd until border measures 1" [2.5 cm]. Break yarn and fasten off.

Weave in ends.

GRAPH A

- ☐ Lt. Blue
- ■ Dk. Blue
- ⧅ Aqua
- ⊙ Natural
- ▣ Camel
- ⊞ Brown
- ☒ Green
- ◪ Dk. Brown
- U Pale Brown

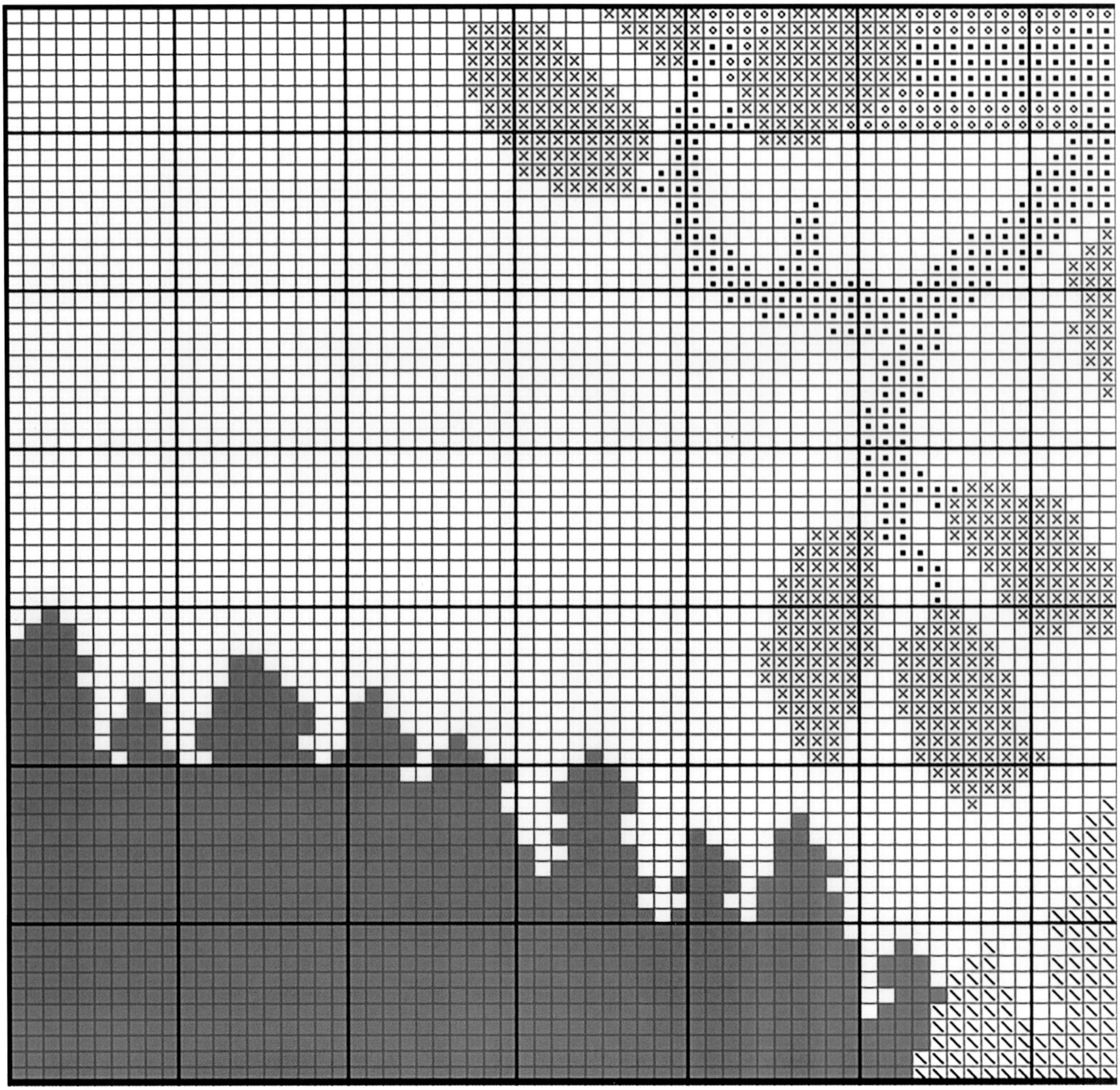

READ WRONG SIDE ROWS FROM THIS SIDE

GRAPH A

Symbol	Color	Symbol	Color
☐	Lt. Blue	+	Brown
■ (shaded)	Dk. Blue	X	Green
\	Aqua	◢	Dk. Brown
○	Natural	U	Pale Brown
▪	Camel		

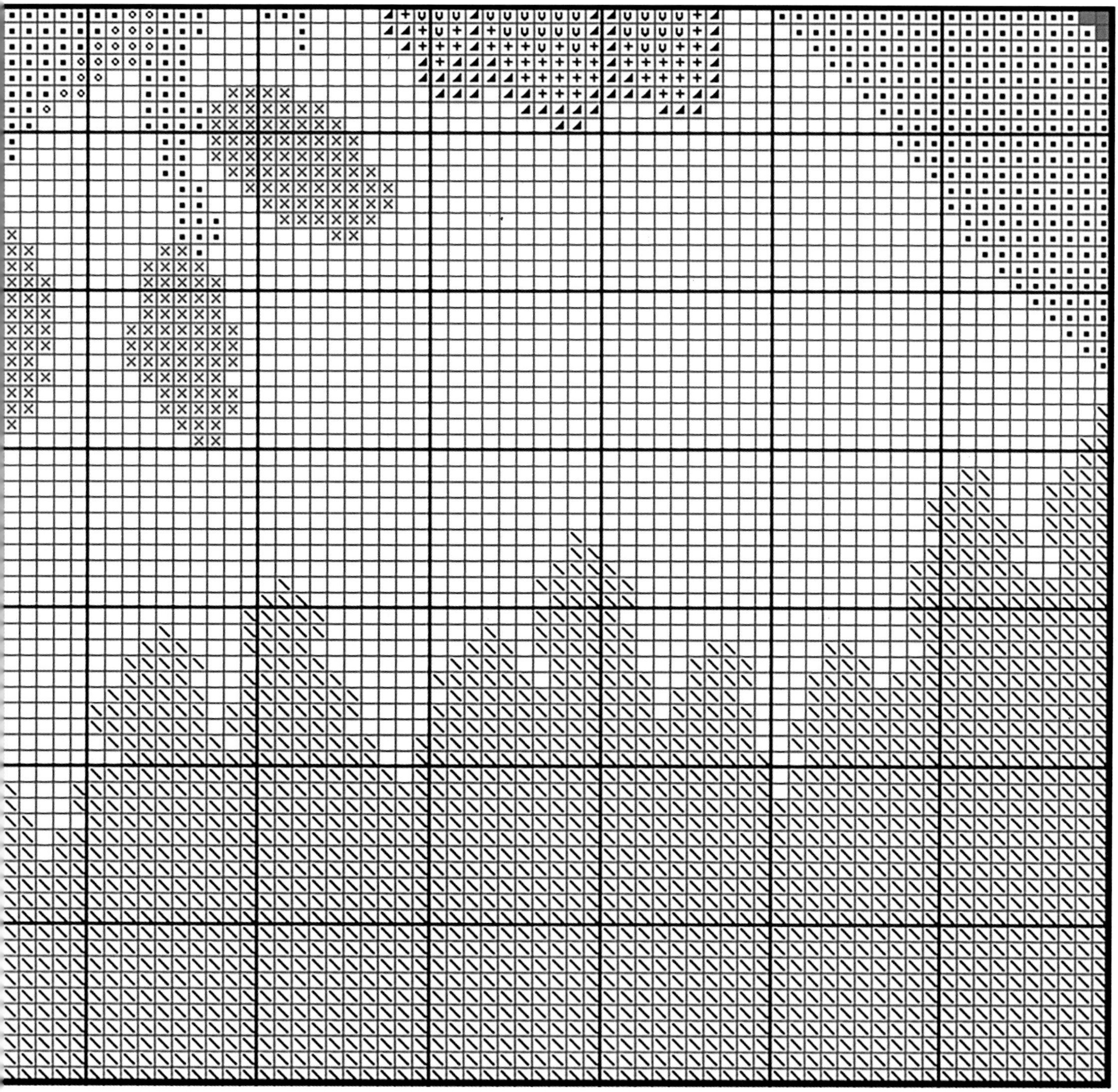

READ RIGHT SIDE ROWS FROM THIS SIDE

GRAPH B

- Lt. Blue
- Dk. Blue
- Natural
- Silver Blue
- Camel
- Brown
- Green
- White
- Dk. Brown
- Dk. Yellow
- Pale Brown
- Yellow
- Taupe Ragg

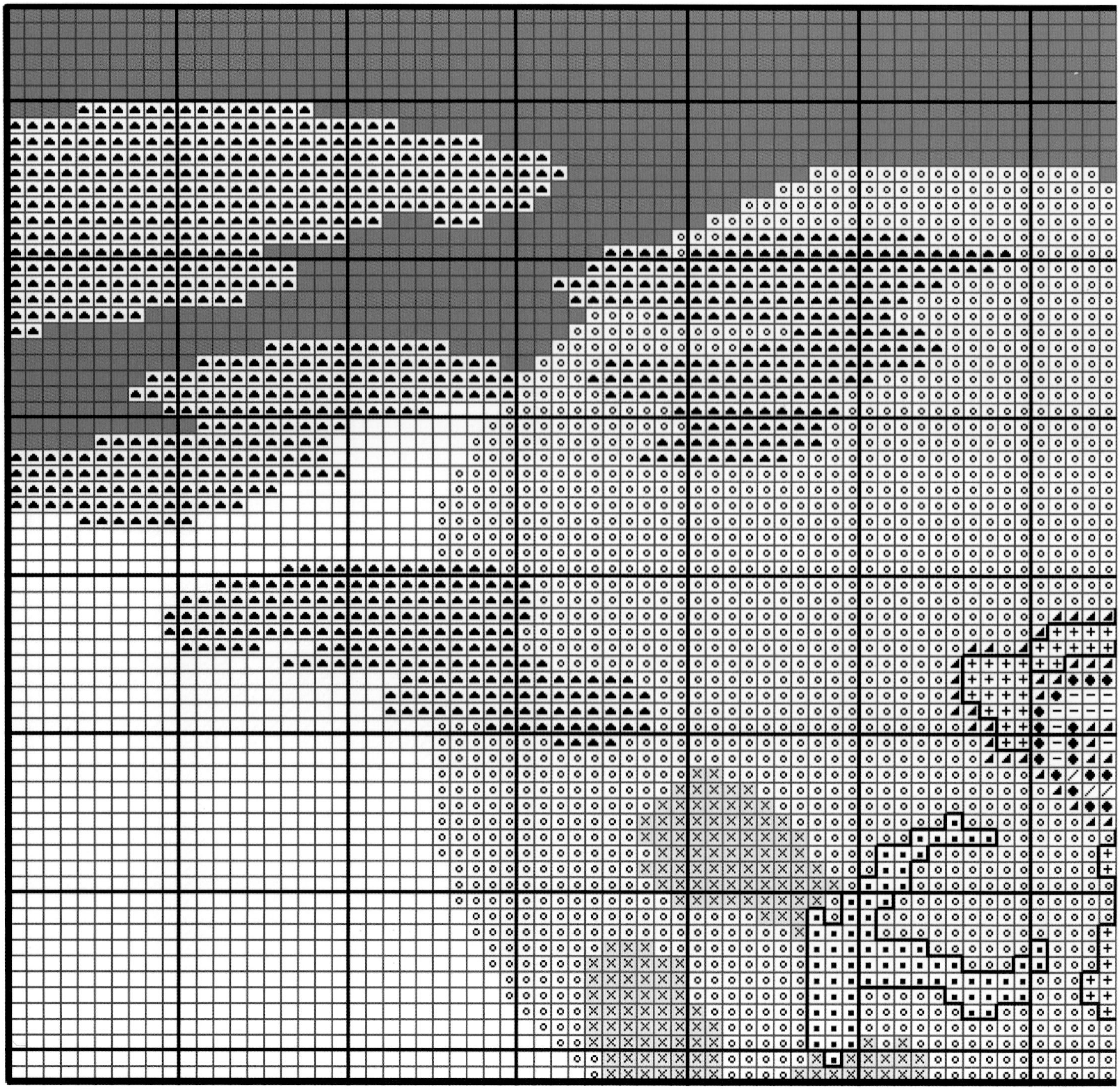

READ WRONG SIDE ROWS FROM THIS SIDE

GRAPH B

- Lt. Blue
- Dk. Blue
- Natural
- Silver Blue
- Camel
- Brown
- Green
- White
- Dk. Brown
- Dk. Yellow
- Pale Brown
- Yellow
- Taupe Ragg

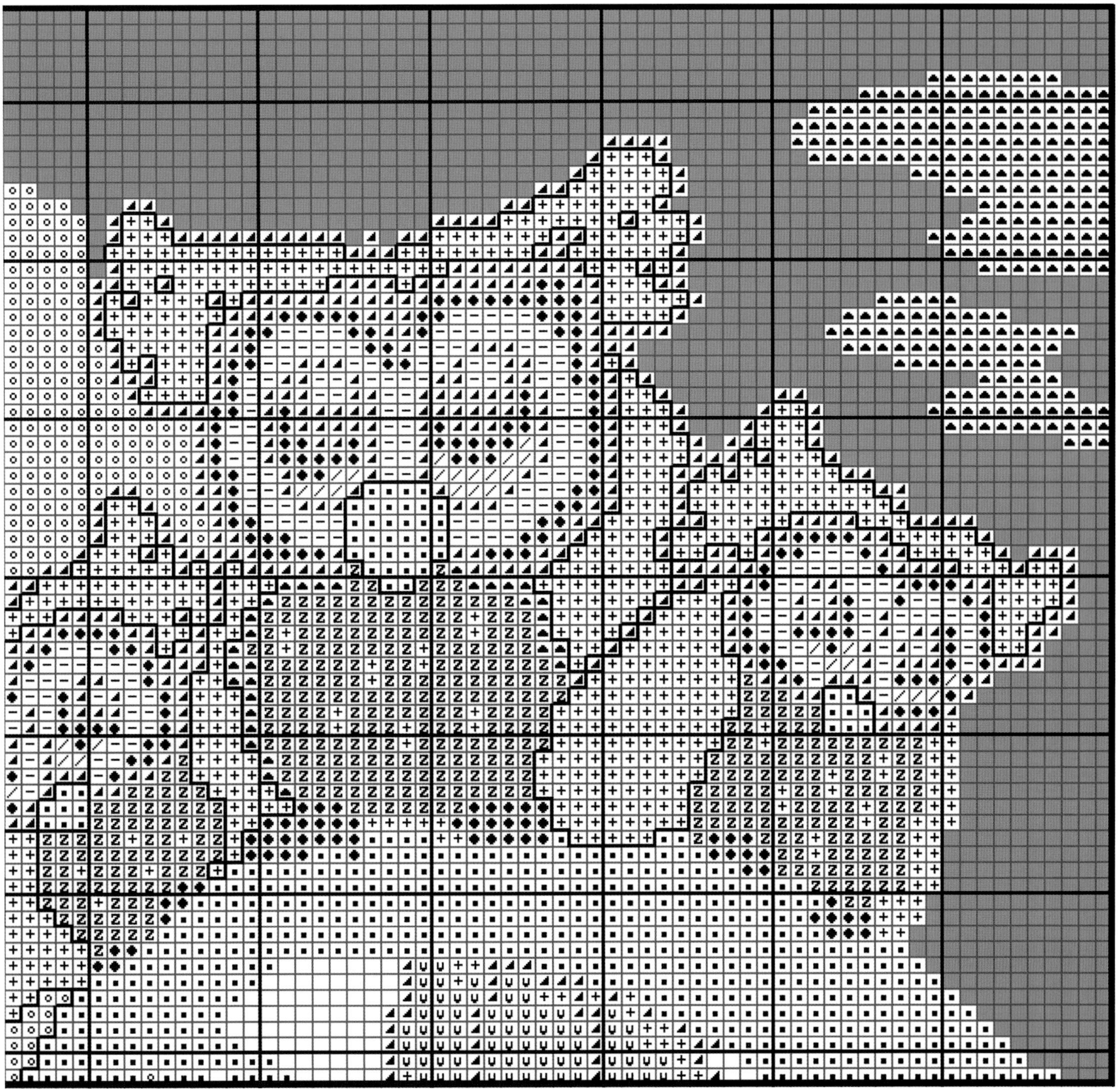

READ RIGHT SIDE ROWS FROM THIS SIDE

Peek-a-Boo Blanket

INTERMEDIATE

SHOPPING LIST

Yarn (Worsted Weight) MEDIUM 4

[3.5 ounces, 180 yards (100 grams, 165 meters) per ball]:

☐ Green	3 balls
☐ Blue	2 balls
☐ Red	2 balls
☐ Yellow	2 balls
☐ Coral	1 ball
☐ Dk. Brown	1 ball
☐ White	1 ball
☐ Pink	70 yds
☐ Golden Brown	70 yds
☐ Lt. Brown	35 yds
☐ Black	35 yds

Crochet Hook

☐ Size J-10 (6.00 mm) or size needed for gauge

SIZE INFORMATION

Size: 38" x 44" [96.5 x 112 cm]

GAUGE INFORMATION

13 sc and 15 rows to 4" [10 cm] measured over single crochet using **suggested** hook or any size hook which will give the correct stitch gauge.

STITCH GUIDE

FPdc- Front Post double crochet: Yo, insert hook from front to back to front around post (or stem) of stitch indicated, yo and draw up a loop, [yo and draw through 2 loops on hook] twice.

Entire afghan is worked in sc. Each square on the graph represents one sc. Color changes are indicated with different symbols. Odd numbered rows or **right side rows** are worked from right to left and even numbered rows or **wrong side rows** are worked from left to right.

To change colors on ODD numbered rows (Right Side Facing): *Work across graph to st before new color, insert hook in next st and pull up a loop; join new color yarn and holding tail at back of work, yarn around hook and pull through 2 loops of previous color on hook.* Notice that the st just made will be entirely in the first color and the loop on the hook in the new color, ready to make the next st. When ready for the next color change, rep from * to *. Old colors are not to be carried across the back of work more than a few sts or you will not have sufficient yarn to complete the afghan. If sts on graph return to original color later in the row, join on a separate ball of yarn. You may need to work with several colors at a time. For large areas of color, use different balls of yarn; for small areas, you can create bobbins of colors needed (allow about 20" [51 cm] for 10 sts). When area of color has been completed, cut yarn leaving a 3-4" [7.5-10 cm] tail to be woven in when afghan has been completed.

A
Boo!
PeeK

To change colors on EVEN numbered rows (Wrong Side Facing): **Work across graph to st before new color, insert hook in next st and pull up a loop, bring strand of yarn to front of work; join new color yarn and holding tail at front of work, yarn around hook and pull through 2 loops on hook.**

NOTE: With both strands of yarn in front at this point, the next sc may be partially hidden - be careful not to skip a st by mistake. When ready for the next color change, rep from ** to **.

If color changes are made correctly, you will be able to see small "feathers" of yarn on the wrong side of work where the old color was brought to the front; but the right side should look quite neat and regular.

INSTRUCTIONS

Using Red, ch 39, change to Coral and ch 40, change to Blue and ch 40 -119 ch.

Foundation Row: Following Row 1 of Graph A on pages 18-19, changing colors as required, sc in 2nd ch from hook and in each ch to end, ch 1, turn -118 sc.

Next Row: Following Row 2 of Graph A, work as follows: sc in first sc and in each sc to end, ch 1, turn - 118 sc.

Repeat last row, but continue to work through Graph A until 76 rows have been completed.

Beg with a right side row, proceed to follow Graph B on pages 20-21, working in the same manner until 76 rows have been completed.

Fasten off.

Weave in all ends.

Please Note: When working border around the outside of the blanket, please note that it is not necessary to work a sc into each stitch at the ends of rows. This may cause the border to be wavy. This border was crocheted by skipping every 3rd or 4th row as needed.

Border:

Rnd 1: With right side of blanket facing, join Dk. Brown with sl st in upper right corner, work 3 sc in same st, work sc spaced evenly around entire outside edge of blanket, working 3 sc in each corner around, join with sl st in first sc.

Rnd 2: Ch 1, sc in each sc around, working 3 sc in center sc of each corner, join with sl st in first sc. Break yarn and fasten off.

Rnd 3: With right side of blanket facing, join Green in center sc of any corner, ch 2 (counts as first hdc throughout), (ch 1, hdc) in same st, *hdc in each sc to center sc of next corner, (hdc, ch 1, hdc) in center sc; rep from * three times more, join with sl st in top of beg hdc.

Rnd 4: Sl st to ch-1 sp, (ch 3, hdc) in same sp, *FPdc around each of next 2 hdc, sc in *back loop only* in each of next 2 hdc; rep from * to ch-1 sp of next corner, adjusting sts to end evenly before corner, (hdc, ch 1, hdc) in corner ch-1 sp; rep from * three times more, join with sl st in 2nd ch of beg ch-3.

Rnd 5: Sl st to ch-1 sp, (ch 3, hdc) in same sp, *sc in back loop of next st, FPdc around each of next 2 FPdc, sc in *back loop only* in each of next 2 sc; rep from * to last st before ch-1 sp of next corner, sc in back loop of next st, (hdc, ch 1, hdc) in corner ch-1 sp; rep from * three times more, join with sl st in 2nd ch of beg ch-3.

Rnd 6: As Rnd 5, but having one more sc before and after each corner. Break yarn and fasten off.

Embroidery: Using White, backstitch Peek A Boo! as indicated on graph.

Backstitch

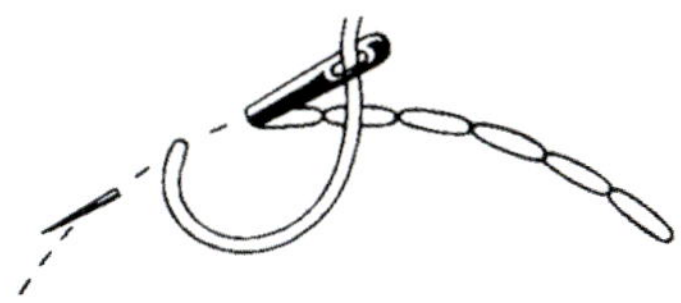

GRAPH A

- Blue
- Pink
- White
- Green
- Red
- Dk Brown
- Golden Brown
- Yellow
- Black
- Lt Brown
- Coral

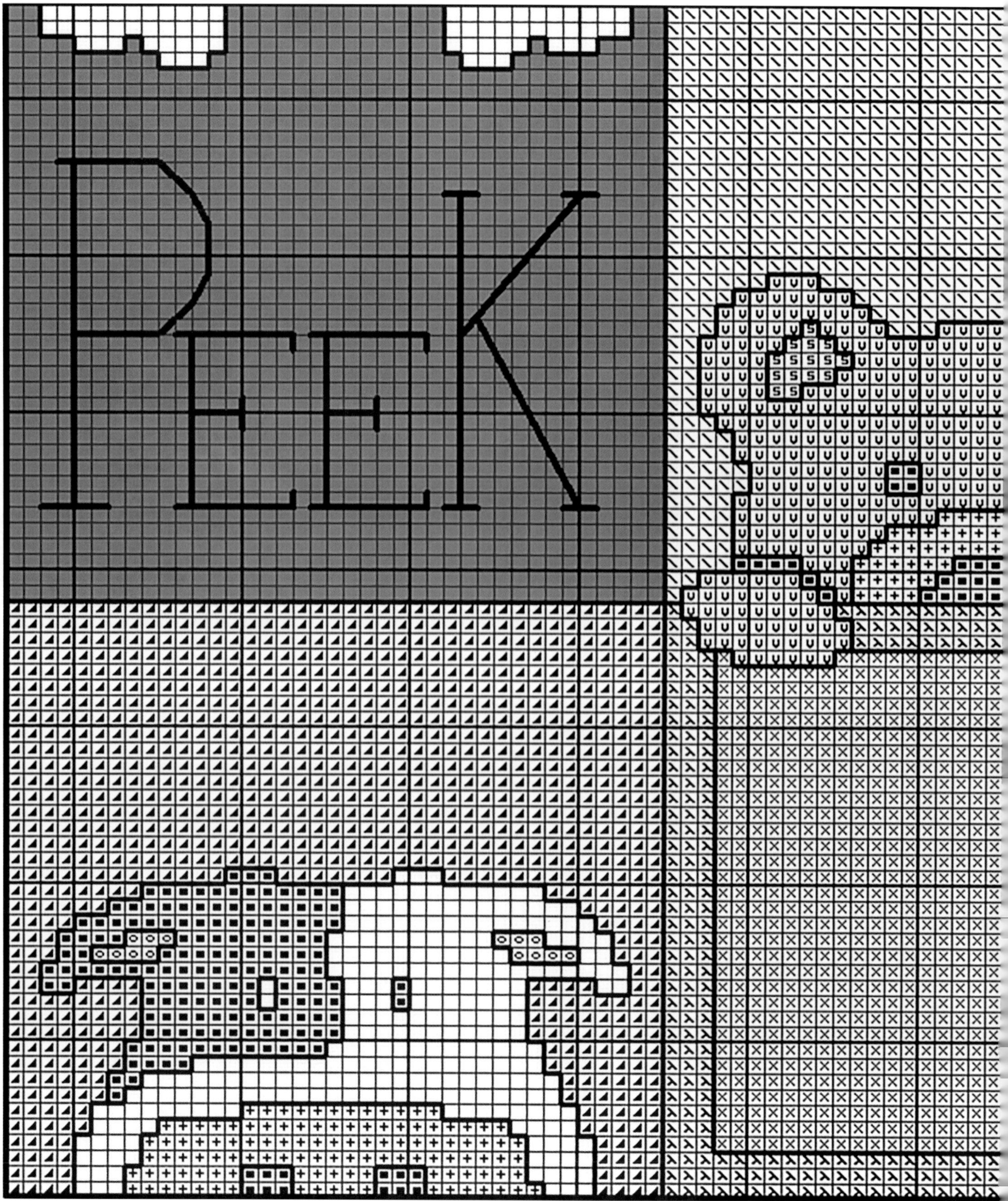

READ WRONG SIDE ROWS FROM THIS SIDE

GRAPH A

Symbol	Color	Symbol	Color	Symbol	Color	Symbol	Color
■ (gray)	Blue	╲	Green	+	Golden Brown	s	Lt Brown
o	Pink	◢	Red	×	Yellow	⅄	Coral
□	White	u	Dk Brown	■	Black		

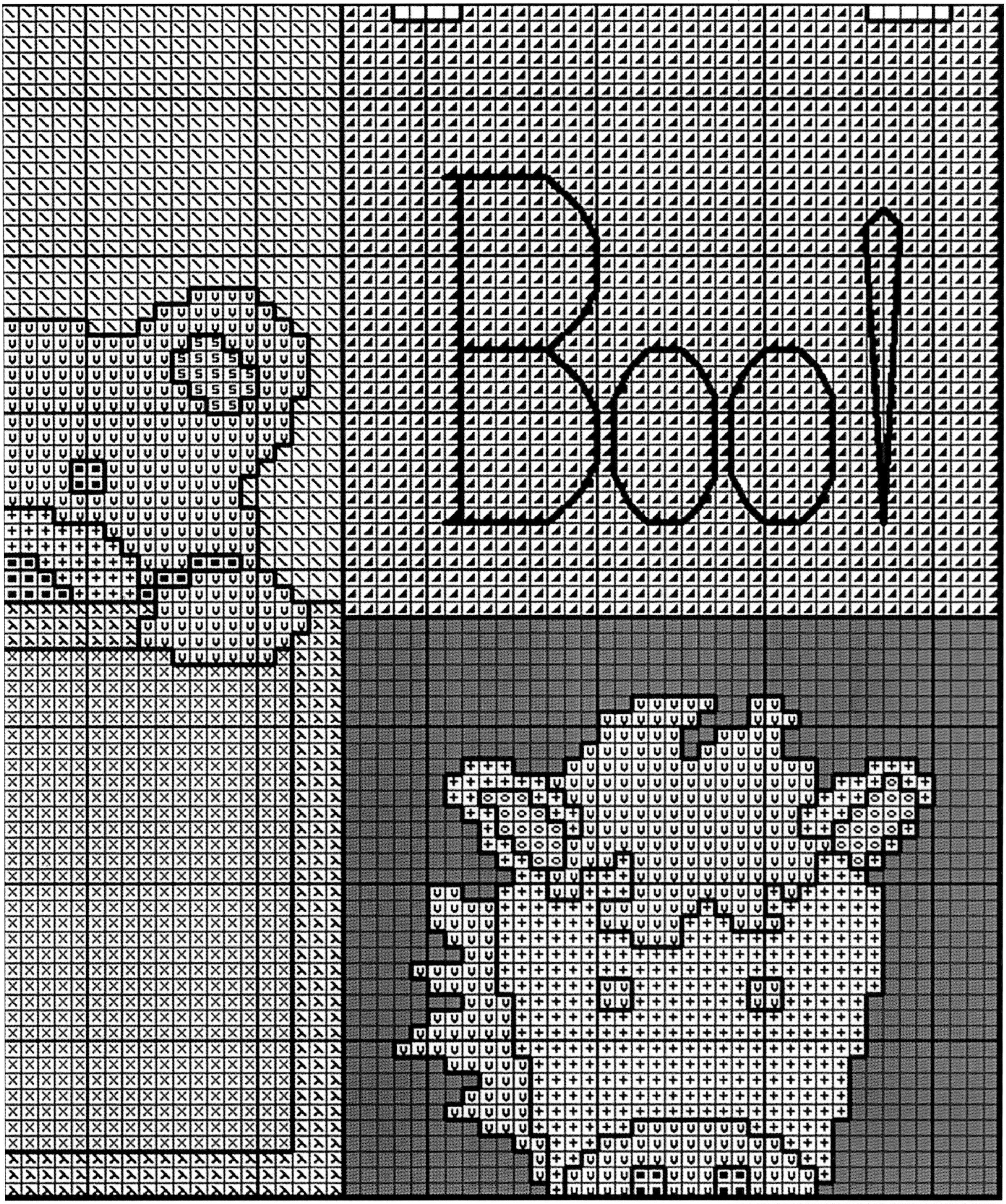

READ RIGHT SIDE ROWS FROM THIS SIDE

GRAPH B

Symbol	Color	Symbol	Color	Symbol	Color	Symbol	Color
■ (shaded)	Blue	╲	Green	+	Golden Brown	5	Lt Brown
o	Pink	◢	Red	×	Yellow	⅄	Coral
□	White	U	Dk Brown	■	Black		

READ WRONG SIDE ROWS FROM THIS SIDE

GRAPH B

- Blue
- Pink
- White
- Green
- Red
- Dk Brown
- Golden Brown
- Yellow
- Black
- Lt Brown
- Coral

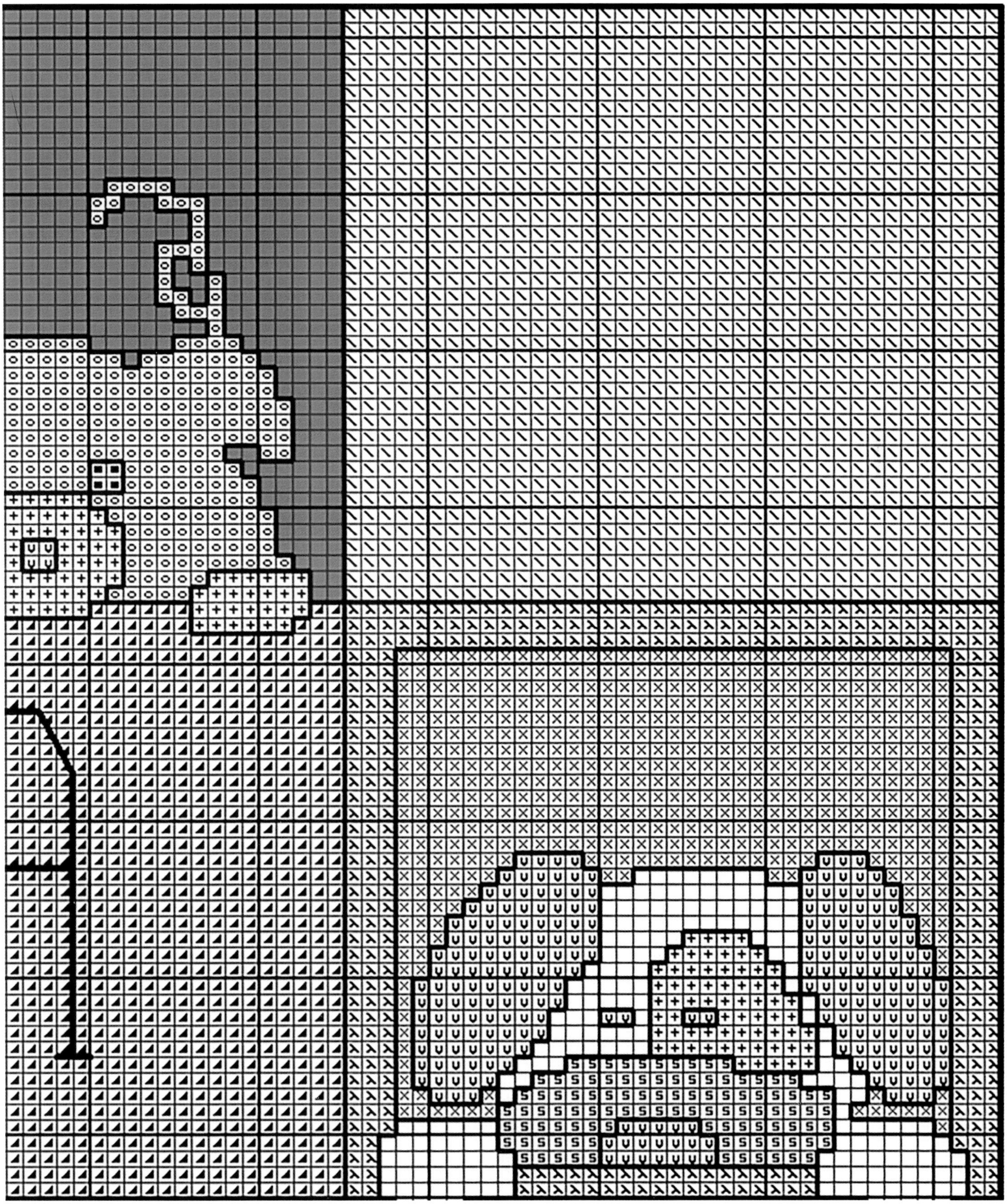

READ RIGHT SIDE ROWS FROM THIS SIDE

General Instructions

ABBREVIATIONS

"	inches
beg	begin or beginning
CC	Contrast Color
ch	chain
cm	centimeters
dc	double crochet
dec	decrease or decreasing
gm	gram
hdc	half double crochet
inc	increase or increasing
MC	Main Color
mm	millimeter(s)
rem	remain or remaining
rep	repeat
rnd(s)	round(s)
sc	single crochet
sl	slip
sp(s)	spaces(s)
st(s)	stitch(es)
tog	together
tr	treble crochet
yo	yarn over hook

*** or **** work instructions following or between * or ** as many more times as indicated in addition to the first time.

() or [ ] work enclosed instructions as many times as specified by the number immediately following or work all enclosed instructions in the stitch or space indicated or contains explanatory remarks

( ) the number(s) given at the end of a row or round denote(s) the number of stitches or spaces you should have on that row or round.

BEGINNER	Projects for first-time crocheters using basic stitches. Minimal shaping.
EASY	Projects using yarn with basic stitches, repetitive stitch patterns, simple color changes, and simple shaping and finishing.
INTERMEDIATE	Projects using a variety of techniques, such as basic lace patterns or color patterns, mid-level shaping and finishing.
EXPERIENCED	Projects with intricate stitch patterns, techniques and dimension, such as non-repeating patterns, multi-color techniques, fine threads, small hooks, detailed shaping and refined finishing.

Yarn Weight Symbol & Names	LACE 0	SUPER FINE 1	FINE 2	LIGHT 3	MEDIUM 4	BULKY 5	SUPER BULKY 6	JUMBO 7
Type of Yarns in Category	Fingering, size 10 crochet thread	Sock, Fingering, Baby	Sport, Baby	DK, Light Worsted	Worsted, Afghan, Aran	Chunky, Craft, Rug	Super Bulky, Roving	Jumbo, Roving
Crochet Gauge* Ranges in Single Crochet to 4" (10 cm)	32-42 sts**	21-32 sts	16-20 sts	12-17 sts	11-14 sts	8-11 sts	6-9 sts	5 sts and fewer
Advised Hook Size Range	Steel*** 6 to 8, Regular hook B-1	B-1 to E-4	E-4 to 7	7 to I-9	I-9 to K-10½	K-10½ to M/N-13	M/N-13 to Q	Q and larger

*GUIDELINES ONLY: The chart above reflects the most commonly used gauges and hook sizes for specific yarn categories.

CROCHET HOOKS													
U.S.	B-1	C-2	D-3	E-4	F-5	G-6	7	H-8	I-9	J-10	K-10½	L-11	M/N-13
Metric - mm	2.25	2.75	3.25	3.5	3.75	4	4.5	5	5.5	6	6.5	8	9

CROCHET TERMINOLOGY		
UNITED STATES		INTERNATIONAL
slip stitch (slip st)	=	single crochet (sc)
single crochet (sc)	=	double crochet (dc)
half double crochet (hdc)	=	half treble crochet (htr)
double crochet (dc)	=	treble crochet (tr)
treble crochet (tr)	=	double treble crochet (dtr)
double treble crochet (dtr)	=	triple treble crochet (ttr)
triple treble crochet (ttr)	=	quadruple treble crochet (qtr)
skip	=	miss

Slip Knot

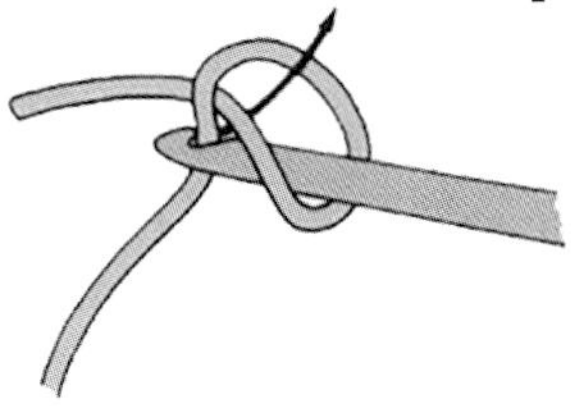

1. Make a loop, then hook another loop through it.

2. Tighten gently and slide the knot up to the hook.

Chain Stitch (ch)

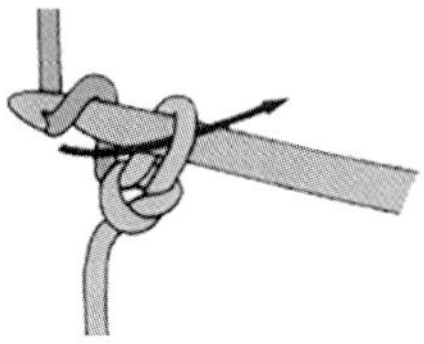

1. Yarn over hook (yo) and draw the yarn through to form a new loop without tightening up the previous one.

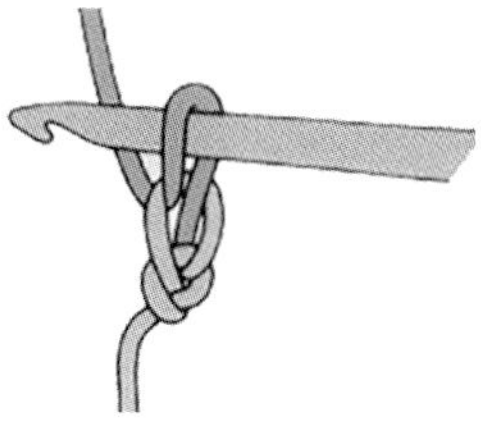

2. Repeat to form as many chains (ch) as required. Do not count the slip knot as a stitch.

Slip Stitch (sl st)

This is the shortest crochet stitch and unlike other stitches is not used on its own to produce a fabric. It is used for joining, shaping and where necessary carrying the yarn to another part of the fabric for the next stage.

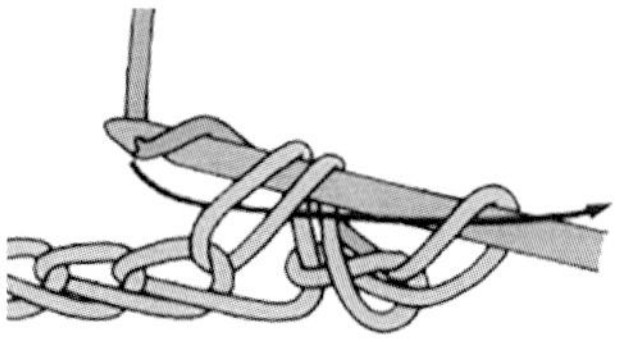

Insert hook into work (second chain from hook), yarn over hook (yo) and draw the yarn through both the work and loop on hook in one movement.

To join a chain ring with a slip stitch (sl st), insert hook into first chain (ch), yarn over hook (yo) and draw through both the work and the yarn on hook in one movement.

Single Crochet (sc)

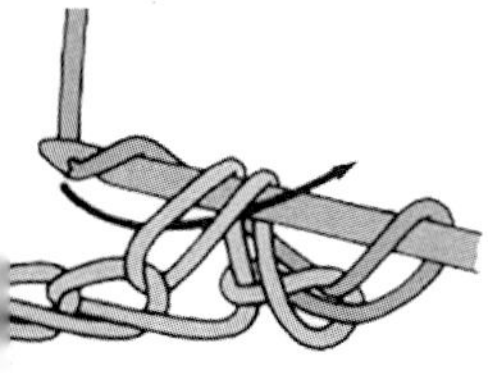

1. Insert the hook into the work (2nd chain (ch) from hook on starting chain), *yarn over hook (yo) and draw yarn through the work only.

2. Yarn over hook (yo) again and draw the yarn through both loops on the hook.

3. 1 single crochet (sc) made. Insert hook into next stitch: repeat (rep) from * in step 1.

Half Double Crochet (hdc)

1. Yarn over hook (yo) and insert the hook into the work (3rd chain (ch) from hook on starting chain) and draw through the work only.

2. Yarn over hook (yo) again and draw through all three loops on the hook.

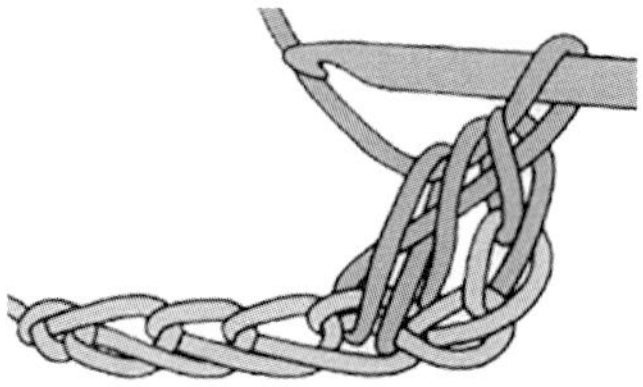

3. 1 hdc made. Yarn over hook (yo), insert hook into next stitch (st) and draw yarn through the work only; repeat (rep) from step 2.

Double Crochet (dc)

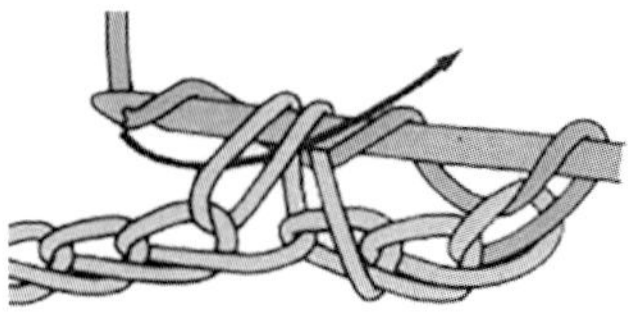

1. Yarn over hook (yo) and insert the hook into the work (4th chain from hook on starting chain) and draw through the work only.

2. Yarn over hook (yo) and draw through the first two loops only.

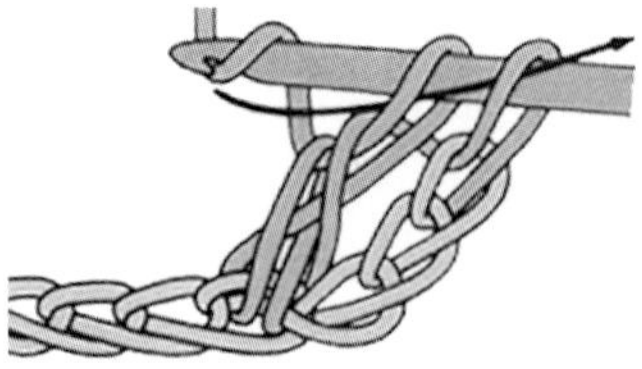

3. Yarn over hook (yo) and draw through the last two loops on the hook.

4. 1 dc made. Yarn over hook (yo), insert hook into next stitch (st) and draw yarn through the work only; repeat (rep) from step 2.

Treble Crochet (tr)

Work same as given for Double Crochet (dc) above,
but in Step 1 yarn over hook (yo) twice, then rep Step 2 twice.

Yarn Information

Projects in this book were made with medium weight yarns. Any brand of yarn may be used. It is best to refer to yardage/meters when determining how many balls or skeins to purchase. Remember, to arrive at the finished size, it is the GAUGE/TENSION that is important, not the brand of yarn. For your convenience, listed below are the specific yarn ranges used to create our photographed models.

Rocking Ponies Blanket
Mary Maxim's Starlette

Night Owls Blanket
Mary Maxim's Starlette

Peek-a-Boo Blanket
Mary Maxim's Starlette

Every effort has been made to have the directions contained in this publication accurate and complete; however, we cannot be responsible for misinterpretation, variance or errors in workmanship of the individual.